TIME
FOR KIDS

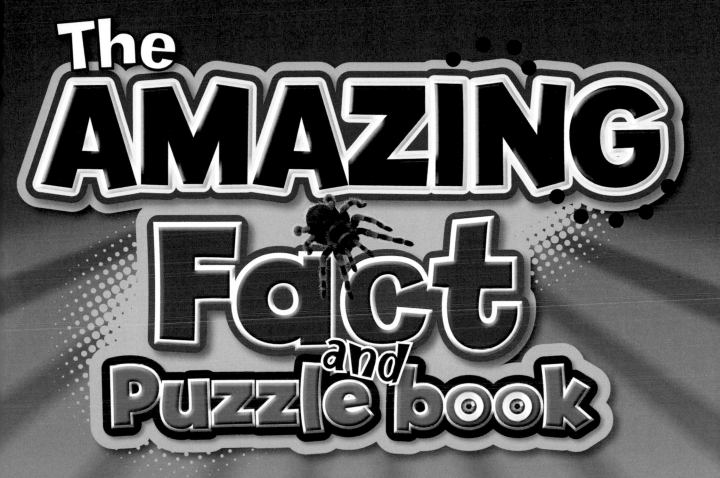

The AMAZING Fact and Puzzle book

Jeff O' Hare

Time Inc. Home Entertainment
Publisher: Richard Fraiman
General Manager: Steven Sandonato
Executive Director, Marketing Services: Carol Pittard
Director, Retail & Special Sales: Tom Mifsud
Director, New Product Development: Peter Harper
Director, Bookazine Marketing: Laura Adam
Publishing Director, Brand Marketing: Joy Butts
Assistant General Counsel: Helen Wan
Associate Marketing Manager: Jonathan White
Design & Prepress Manager: Anne-Michelle Gallero
Book Production Manager: Susan Chodakiewicz
Associate Prepress Manager: Alex Voznesenskiy
Assistant Book Production Manager: Brynn Joyce

TIME For Kids
Managing Editor: Nellie Gonzalez Cutler
Editor, Time Learning Ventures: Jonathan Rosenbloom

Created by **Q2AMedia**
Publishing Director: Chester Fisher
Editor: Charles and Linda George
Sr. Art Director: Rahul Dhiman
Cover Design: Harleen Mehta
Designers: Gaurav Arora, Neha Kaul
Picture Researchers: Anju Pathak, Anubhav Singhal, Nivisha Sinha

Special Thanks to:
Christine Austin, Jeremy Biloon, Alexandra Bliss, Glenn Buonocore, Jim Childs, Rose Cirrincione, Jacqueline Fitzgerald, Carrie Frazier, Lauren Hall, Jennifer Jacobs, Suzanne Janso, Mona Li, Robert Marasco, Amy Migliaccio, Brooke Reger, Dave Rozzelle, Ilene Schreider, Adriana Tierno, Sydney Webber

Time Inc.
1271 Avenue of the Americas
New York, New York 10020

ISBN 13: 978-1-60320-841-3
ISBN 10: 1-60320-841-0

TIME For Kids Books is a trademark of Time Inc.

We welcome your comments and suggestions about TIME For Kids Books.
Please write to us at:
TIME For Kids Books
Attention: Book Editors
PO Box 11016
Des Moines, IA 50336-1016

If you would like to order any of our hardcover Collector's Edition books, please call us at 1-800-327-6388.
(Monday through Friday, 7:00 a.m.— 8:00 p.m. or Saturday, 7:00 a.m.— 6:00 p.m. Central Time).

1 WCD 10

Picture credits
t = top, b = bottom, c = center, r = right, l = left

Cover Image: Pyshnyy Maxim Vjacheslavovich/Shutterstock, Shutterstock, Feraru Nicolae/Shutterstock, Radek Smrcka/Shutterstock, Shutterstock

Back Cover Image: Craigrjd/Dreamstime, Jurie Maree /Shutterstock, George Toubalis/Shutterstock, Luis Castro/Shutterstock, Sakala/Shutterstock, Shutterstock

Title Page: Shutterstock

Insides: Craigrjd/Dreamstime: 6t, Pyshnyy Maxim Vjacheslavovich/Shutterstock: 6b, Mircea Bezergheanu/Shutterstock: 7l, Levent Konuk/Shutterstock: 7r, Lucian Coman/Shutterstock: 7b, PhotoSky/Shutterstock: 8t, Susan Flashman/123rf: 8c, Fivespots/Shutterstock, ZanyZeus/Shutterstock: 8b, Armin Rose/Shutterstock: 9t, Gentoo Multimedia Ltd./Shutterstock, FloridaStock/Shutterstock: 9b, Docwhite/Nature Picture Library: 10t, Abraham Badenhorst/Shutterstock: 10b, Yuri Arcurs/Shutterstock: 11tl, OAR/National Undersea Research Program: 11tr, David Shale/Nature Picture Library: 11c, Dante Fenolio/Science Photo Library: 11b, Smellme/Dreamstime: 12t, Ashims/Shutterstock: 12b, Shane White/Shutterstock: 13t, Ewan Chesser/Dreamstime: 13b, Creations/Shutterstock: 14-15, Red Frog/Istockphoto: 14, Christian Musat/Shutterstock, Mandy Godbehear/Shutterstock: 15t, Shutterstock: 15b, Christos Georghiou/Shutterstock: 16-17, Yuri Shirokov/Shutterstock: 16t, Elena Stepanova/Dreamstime: 16b, David Fisher/Rex Features, BDG/Rex Features, Michael Williams/Rex Features, Charles Sykes/Rex Features: 17t, Elena Stepanova/Dreamstime: 17c, Elena Stepanova/Dreamstime: 17br, Creations/Shutterstock: 18-19, Newphotoservice/Shutterstock: 18t, Henrik Jonsson/Istockphoto: 18b, Sofia Santos/Shutterstock: 19t, Max Delson Martins Santos: 19c, Benjamin Albiach Galan: 19b, Feraru Nicolae/Shutterstock: 20l,Tan, Kim Pin/Shutterstock: 20r,Tiplyashin Anatoly/Shutterstock: 21tl, Alhovik/Shutterstock: 21tr, Matt Kunz/Istockphoto: 21c, Jon le-Bon/Shutterstock: 20-21, Donald R. Swartz/Shutterstock: 20-21, Pichugin Dmitry/Shutterstock: 21-22, Shutterstock: 22t,Timo Kohlbacher/Shutterstock: 22bl, Hydromet/Shutterstock: 22br, Radek Smrcka/Shutterstock: 23t, Chris Jackson/WPA Pool /Getty Images: 24t, David Hartley/Rex Features: 24br, Keo/Shutterstock: 24-25, Rui Saraiva/Shutterstock: 25l, Rex Features: 25r, Stacey Lynn Payne/Shutterstock: 26-27, Andrew F. Kazmierski/Shutterstock: 26t, Luciano Mortula/Shutterstock: 26b, Stacey Lynn Payne/Shutterstock: 27t, Vinicius Tupinamba/Shutterstock: 27b, Wong Yu Liang/Shutterstock, Donald R. Swartz/Shutterstock: 28-29, Sam Dcruz/Shutterstock: 28, Dusan Po/Shutterstock, Adam.Golabek/Shutterstock, Fenton/Shutterstock: 29, Hfng/Shutterstock: 30-31, Olga Besnard/Shutterstock: 30t, Roberto Romanin/Shutterstock: 30bl, Luis Castro/Shutterstock: 30br, Alex Staroseltsev/Shutterstock: 31t, Vladimir Korostyshevskiy/Shutterstock: 31b, Nuka/Shutterstock: 31t, Reto Stöckli, Nazmi El Saleous, and Marit Jentoft-Nilsen/NASA GSFC: 32l, Samuel Acosta/Shutterstock: 32r, Zacarias Pereira Da Mata/Shutterstock: 34-35, Jim Jurica/Istockphoto: 34t, Stéphane Bidouze/Shutterstock: 34b, Warren Goldswain/Shutterstock: 35t, Dudarev Mikhail/Shutterstock: 35bl, Robert F. Balazik/Shutterstock: 35br, Michael Gray/Big Stock Photo: 36t, Sakala/Shutterstock: 36b, Martin D. Vonka/Shutterstock: 37t, Terrance Emerson/Shutterstock: 37b, George Toubalis/Shutterstock: 38-39, Graça Victoria/Shutterstock: 38t, Dwight Smith/Shutterstock: 38b, Jurie Maree/Shutterstock: 39t, Rich Carey/Shutterstock: 39b, Brenton Hodgson/Shutterstock: 40-41, My Summit/Shutterstock: 40, Thoron/Shutterstock: 41t, Cosmopolyt/Dreamstime: 41b, GoodMood Photo/Shutterstock: 42-43, Alastair Pidgen /Imagine Images/ Shutterstock: 42, Ron Hilton/Shutterstock: 43t, Kavram/Shutterstock: 43b, Javarman/Shutterstock, Galyna Andrushko/Shutterstock: 44-45, Galyna Andrushko/Shutterstock: 45t, Robyn Mackenzie/Big Stock Photo: 45b, B.G. Smith/Shutterstock, Ekaterina Pokrovskaya/Shutterstock: 46-47, Iamanewbee/Shutterstock: 47t, Goddard Space Flight Center/ NASA: 47b, Ymgerman/Istockphoto, Khomulo Anna/Shutterstock: 48-49, Joy Stein/Shutterstock: 48t, Jan Martin Will/Shutterstock: 48b, Shutterstock: 49, Andrew N. Ilyasov/Shutterstock: 50-51, Ttphoto/Shutterstock: 50t, Shutterstock: 50bl, Shutterstock: 50br, Jan Martin Will/Shutterstock: 51, Viktoriya/Shutterstock: 52-53, North Wind Pictures/Photolibrary: 52t, Photolibrary: 52b, Lebrecht Music & Arts Photo Library/Photolibrary: 53l, Steven Wynn/Photolibrary: 53r, Mary Evans Picture Library/Photolibrary: 54t, OAR/National Undersea Research Program(NURP) Woods Hole Oceanographic Inst./NOAA: 54b, Grafissimo/Istockphoto: 55b, Argus/Shutterstock: 56-57, Capital Pictures: 56t, Rex Features: 56bl, Capital Pictures: 56br, Capital Pictures: 57t, Rex features: 57b, Kentoh/Shutterstock: 58-59, C.Paramount/Everett/Rex Features: 58t, Capital Pictures: 58c,58cl,58cr, Angello Picco/Rex Features: 58b, C.Foxsearch/Everett/Rex Features: 59, Gino Santa Maria/Shutterstock: 60-61, Everett Collection/Rex Features: 60t, C.20thC.Fox/Everett/Rex Features: 60b, Everett Collection/Rex Features: 61t, C.20thC.Fox/Everett/Rex Features: 61b, Dwphotos/Shutterstock: 62-63, Fotos International/Rex Features: 62t, Laurent Renault/Shutterstock: 62br, Morlock/Shutterstock: 62bl, Keo/Shutterstock: 63, Albert Michael/Rex Features: 63t, Newspix/Rex Features: 63c, Andre Csillag/Rex Features: 63b, Kundra/Shutterstock: 64-65, Ilpo Musto/Rex Features: 64t, Pavel K/Shutterstock: 64b, Brian J. Ritchie/Rex Features: 65t, Lucas Jackson/Reuters: 65b, Albo/Shutterstock: 66-67, J. Helgason/Shutterstock, Sabri Deniz Kizil/Shutterstock, Richard Clement/Reuters: 66t, AP Photo: 66c, Albo/Shutterstock, Kirill R/Shutterstock: 67, Roberto Schmidt/AFP: 67r, FotoManijak/Shutterstock: 68-69, Trinacria Photo/Shutterstock, Donald Miralle/Getty Images: 68t, David Wilkinson/Rex Features, Ron Sachs/Rex Features: 68c, Sportsphotographer. eu/Shutterstock: 69t, Pete Niesen/Shutterstock: 69c, Graphic Design/Shuttrestock: 70-71, Pixinity/Shutterstock: 70, Felinda/Dreamstime: 71, Stocksnapp/Shutterstock: 72-73, John Verner/Istockphoto: 72, Katherine Welles/Shutterstock: 73t, Keith Binns/Istockphoto: 73b, Galyna Andrushko/ Shutterstock: 74-75, King Ho

Contents

Answers to the puzzles are at the back of the book 78

VERTEBRATES

SHOW SOME BACKBONE

Vertebrates are animals with spines, or backbones. Imagine how hard it would be to walk without one! The spine supports the skeleton, which supports muscles, ligaments, and other body parts. Bundles of nerves run up and down the spine, carrying information from the brain to the body, and vice versa.

Bats are the only mammals that truly fly. Their backbones give their bodies stability in flight.

Thank You, Spine!

Having a spine helps animals develop bigger brains. Vertebrates are the smartest animals, so if you can read this, thank your spine!

01 PUZZLE
★★☆☆☆

Find Four

The names of four animals in this category can be found scrambled in the letters VERTEBRATE. Not all letters will be used.

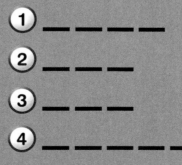

1. ___ ___ ___ ___
2. ___ ___ ___
3. ___ ___ ___
4. ___ ___ ___ ___ ___ ___

INVERTEBRATES

SPINELESS!

Invertebrates are animals without spines. These include sponges, scorpions, spiders, jellyfish, worms, mollusks, bees, lobsters, octopi, and many more. In fact, 95% of animals don't have spines.

Jellyfish aren't fish. They're not jelly, either. They're mostly water, and they don't even have a brain.

The tentacles on some jellyfish can sting you!

They're Everywhere!
Invertebrates crawl, fly, float, or swim in almost all of Earth's habitats! Be careful, or you'll step on one!

Tarantulas look scary, but some people think they make pretty good pets. Treat them gently, though. They can bite.

02 PUZZLE
★★☆☆☆

Letter Web

Follow the lines to place the letters into the correct boxes and you will reveal the name of a major invertebrate.

A A A A L N R T T U

TFK

WHAT KIND OF -THERM ARE YOU?

COLD-BLOODED

COLD COMFORT

Fish, insects, amphibians, and reptiles are ectotherms. That means they're cold-blooded. Because they can't regulate their body temperature, it matches the air around them. In hot environments, their blood is warm. In cold ones, it's cold. If it's really cold, they can't move at all. They become torpid. What a great word!

Torpid?
Torpor is temporary hibernation. Cold-blooded animals can't move fast when it's cold. They become torpid.

Crocodiles use their massive tails as a paddle, a rudder, and a weapon—when hunting or when threatened.

03 ★★★★★ PUZZLE

Hop To It

Can you move all of the frogs on the left to the right and all of the frogs on the right to the left? Each frog may only move forward to an empty space OR it may jump over one frog in front if there is an empty space on the other side. You may use pennies or markers on the page to keep track of movement. If you can't solve this right away, don't give up. It's a challenge!

WARM-BLOODED

WARM WONDERS

Mammals and birds are endotherms. That means they're warm-blooded. Food they eat converts into energy to keep them warm, no matter how cold it is outside. Warm-blooded animals move easily in climates where cold-blooded animals can barely move at all.

Seals can live in cold climates because they're warm-blooded, and because they have a thick layer of fat for insulation.

HOME, iCY HOME
Seals and penguins live in the southern hemisphere, especially along the coast of Antarctica.

04 PUZZLE

Snow Problem

Penguins and polar bears are two animals that can live in extreme temperatures. Do you notice anything unusual about this picture?

Hint:
Polar bears live in the Arctic. Where do penguins live?

TFK

DEEP SEA DISCOVERIES

WONDERS WAY DOWN UNDER

Huge critters—and very tiny ones—live in the deep ocean. A giant squid can grow to 60 feet (18 m) long! This "sea monster" can attack a whale and eat the whole thing! Chemotrophs are tiny bacteria that live near thermal vents—mini-volcanoes—way down on the ocean floor. In between, there are animals of all sizes and shapes— octopus, crab, shrimp, and lots of strange-looking fish.

A viperfish's teeth are so long, they won't fit in its mouth!

Vampire Squid
The vampire squid has tentacles that look like vampire teeth.

05 PUZZLE
★★☆☆☆

Spot It

Animals sometimes camouflage themselves. Their colors or shapes blend into their surroundings, hiding them. Can you find the animal camouflaged here?

Deep Trouble

GHOTIO isn't really a word, but when you pronounce parts of it like parts of 'enough,' 'women,' and 'caution,' it sounds like something you'd find in the sea. Can you figure out what it is?

CAUTION

Giant tube worms live on the deep ocean floor, in water so toxic it would kill you in a minute!

LOOK OUT BELOW!

Some deep sea creatures create their own light. A lantern fish has tentacles that look like tiny worms hanging above its head. It sits really still, and when a smaller fish tries to eat the "worms," the lantern fish gobbles it up! Some deep-sea shrimp can vomit glowing goo to scare away predators. Gross! And a vampire squid squirts a glowing cloud of icky stuff to keep predators away.

The anglerfish has a glowing spine on its head. The fish wiggles this spine to lure its prey.

Going Fishing

Another deep sea fish, the humpback angler fish, or blackdevil, has a sort of fishing lure on its nose to attract prey.

A firefly squid is the only member of the squid family that can see colors.

TFK

WEIRD AND WILD

Aye-ayes live high in the trees of Madagascar and eat insects. These big-eyed cuties look like they belong to the bat family, but they're actually related to monkeys and humans.

The aye-aye uses its fingers and thumbs sort of like humans, to grasp things. It uses its long middle fingers for digging.

07 PUZZLE

Platy-Pieces

A platypus looks like it was mixed together from lots of other animals. See if you can name an animal that might resemble each part of the platypus.

Bill

Tail

Skin or fur

Mixed-up Animal
The platypus lays eggs like a bird! It has poisonous spurs on its hind legs, and its name means "flat-foot."

AUSTRALIA RULES!

Australia is home to lots of weird critters. Echidnas have long snouts and tiny, toothless mouths. They roll themselves into spiny balls when they're scared. A platypus is a crazy-looking animal that lays eggs. It grinds its food by putting pebbles and gravel into its toothless mouth. Tasmanian devils have awfully bad breath! They eat dead animals.

Echidna

Tasmanian devils are really ferocious, and when they screech at night, it's scary!

Dig it!
Wombats can dig a hole faster than a person who's using a shovel.

08 **PUZZLE**

Scramble

Each of these words can be unscrambled to reveal the name of an unusual animal. How many can you find?

oakla

angoorak

chostir

RATTLE AROUND IN YOUR BONES

NO BONES ABOUT IT!

Bones provide a framework for your muscles, your internal organs, and your skin. The rib cage keeps your lungs and heart safe when you bump into something. When you bump your head, your skull keeps your soft brain from getting mashed. The longest bone in your body is the femur, in your upper leg. Your smallest bone is the stirrup, in your ear.

Where'd They Go?

At birth, babies have over 300 bones, while adults have only 206. Some bones in newborns fuse together as they grow.

A BONE TO PICK

Bones look hard, but they grow with you, from the time you're born until you become an adult. Bones store vitamins, minerals, and chemicals your body needs to grow. Your body needs calcium to help maintain bone strength and structure. Without calcium, they'd get brittle—like chalk—and break. That's no fun!

Human thigh bones—femurs—are, pound for pound, stronger than concrete.

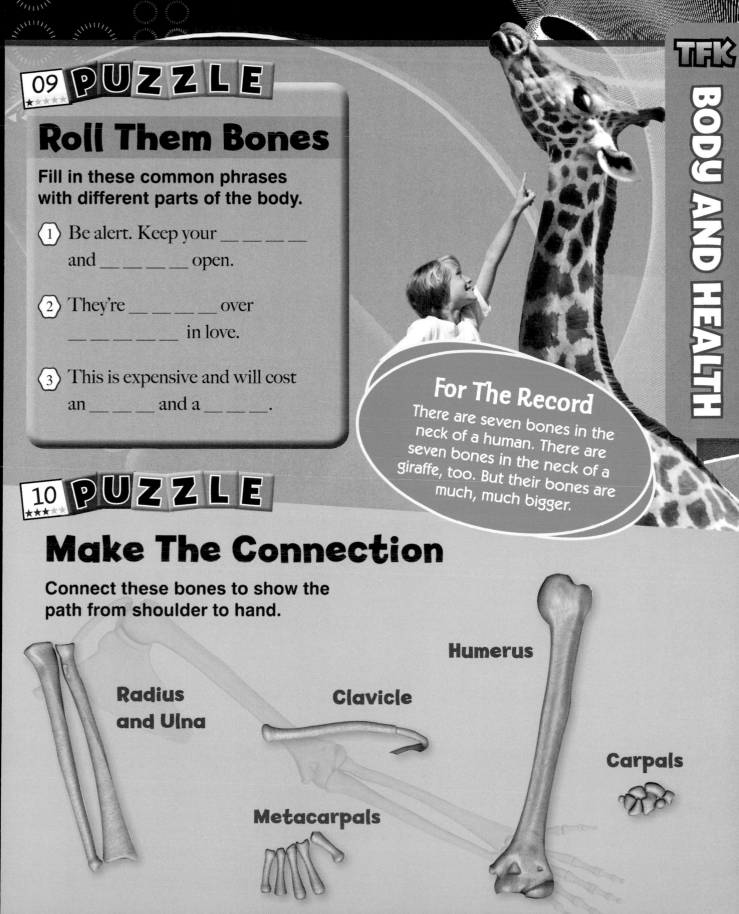

09 PUZZLE

Roll Them Bones

Fill in these common phrases with different parts of the body.

1. Be alert. Keep your __ __ __ __ __ and __ __ __ __ __ open.

2. They're __ __ __ __ __ over __ __ __ __ __ __ in love.

3. This is expensive and will cost an __ __ __ __ and a __ __ __ __.

For The Record

There are seven bones in the neck of a human. There are seven bones in the neck of a giraffe, too. But their bones are much, much bigger.

10 PUZZLE

Make The Connection

Connect these bones to show the path from shoulder to hand.

Humerus

Radius and Ulna

Clavicle

Carpals

Metacarpals

COME TO YOUR SENSES

Humans have **five senses**.

They Really Have Taste!

Some people have a highly-developed sense of taste. They taste foods like coffee, soda pop, and chocolate for a living.

11 PUZZLE
★★★☆☆

A Code In The Nose

To find the name of the condition where someone has lost the sense of smell, solve this tricky code. You must go back along the alphabet the number of letters that match the position of the letter in the word given. In other words, for the first letter, you go back one letter in the alphabet. For the second letter, go back two letters, three letters for the third, and so on.

B P R W R O H

___ ___ ___ ___ ___ ___ ___

We **hear** when vibrations hit our eardrums and tiny bones called the hammer, stirrup, and anvil in our middle ears.

Compensation

When a person becomes disabled and loses one of the senses, the other four may get more sensitive. People who become blind, for example, usually develop very good hearing, and their sense of touch allows them to read Braille.

We **see** because light hits the retina, a tiny screen in the back of our eyeballs. Images speed from there to the brain.

Eye-Eye

Can you identify the owners of these eyes?

Remember That Smell?

Memory can be strongly linked to the sense of smell. What do you think of when you smell cookies baking?

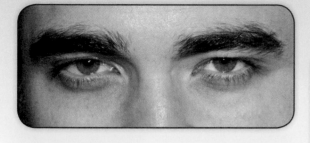

We have **taste** buds on our tongues that perk up when food plops down on them.

We **smell** tiny molecules of freshly-baked cookies that have drifted through the air, entered our nose, and tickled receptor cells that sent the smells on to our brain.

When we **touch** something, nerves in our skin send messages really fast to our brain, which figures out if the object is soft or hard, rough or smooth, or hot or cold.

STRANGE
BUT TRUE

Cell-abrate!

Humans start life as a single cell. It splits and splits, until there are millions of cells. "Voila!"—a baby! All cells are pretty much living things. In fact, some living things are made up entirely of a single cell.

Stem cells are cells in the body that can become anything—muscles, nerves, organs, or skin. That makes them special! Scientists are hoping to use stem cells to produce muscle and nerve tissue, and possibly someday even organs for transplantation.

A human egg cell divides again and again to form a blastocyst—hundreds of cells—that eventually becomes a person!

13 PUZZLE

Three's a Charm!

Can you name at least 10 body parts that can be spelled using only three letters? We've done one for you.

1. _____Eye_____
2. _____
3. _____
4. _____
5. _____
6. _____
7. _____
8. _____
9. _____
10. _____

This is how you'd look without your skin. Cool, huh? Gross, too!

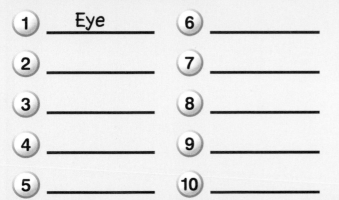

THE BAFFLING BODY

Did you know that you can't control one of your strongest muscles? Your heart is an involuntary muscle, and you never have to think about it. It beats whether you're awake or asleep. Your heart has a big job to do, too. It pumps more than 2,000 gallons (7,570.8 L) of blood around your body every day!

A healthy heart beats about 2.6 billion times during a person's lifetime!

14 PUZZLE

DNA

The letters D, N, or A have been removed from these words. Can you put the letters back in to complete the name of each body part? You can use the letters more than once in a word.

1. B R _ I _
2. K I _ _ E Y
3. T E _ _ O _
4. H _ _ _

Lots of Power in a Small Package

Did you know that your heart is about as big as your fist? It's odd that something that small can work that hard.

19

SCRAPING THE SKY

When the Empire State Building was completed in 1931, it was the world's tallest building. From base to tip, its architectural height (which doesn't include the antenna on the roof) is 1,250 feet (381 m). Now, it's not in the top 10. The recently completed Burj Khalifa Tower, in Dubai, United Arab Emirates, is twice as tall, based on the same standards of measurement. It's the tallest man-made structure ever built—2,717 feet (828 m) tall. That's more than half a mile straight up!

BIG BOYS

Until the Burj Khalifa Tower was built, the tallest building in the world was the Taipei 101 in Taiwan—1,671 feet (509 m). The building with the highest occupied floor for offices is the Shanghai World Financial Center. Imagine looking out your office window from 1,614 ft (492 m) up!

On New Year's Eve, 2009, approximately 22,000 fireworks were fired from the sides and top of Taipei 101, lighting up the skies of the city.

According to the website http://www.emporis.com, these are the 10 tallest buildings in the world.

600m (1,968 feet)
500m (1,640 feet)
400m (1,312 feet)
300m (984 feet)
200m (656 feet)
100m (328 feet)
0m

Burj Khalifa, Dubai, United Arab Emirates

Taipei 101, Taiwan

Shanghai World Financial Center, Shanghai

Petronas Tower 1 & 2, Kuala Lumpur

Nanjing Greenland Financial Center, China

Willis Tower, Chicago, Illinois

Guangzhou West Tower, China

Jin Mao Tower, Shanghai

Two International Finance Centre, Hong Kong

The needle-shaped tower on top of the Burj Khalifa may be visible from as far as 60 miles (96.6 km) away.

TFK

15 PUZZLE
★★★★

High Life

★HINT:
This TV personality's first name.

Follow this picture puzzle to find the name of the man who, in 1974, walked a high wire between the unfinished Twin Towers in New York City, at a height of 1,368 ft (417.0 m) above the ground.

First Name: 🧑 + Y - ZR = _____

Last Name: 🌼 - AL + IT = _____

Dubai City
Dubai City, located at the southern end of the Persian Gulf, is the capital of one of the seven emirates included in the United Arab Emirates. Dubai City is one of the fastest growing cities in the world.

16 PUZZLE
★★★★★

"Tall" Order?

Take a little time to join these dots together in the order given. When completed, you will reveal the U.S. state whose capital has the word "tall" in its name.

	A	B	C	D	E	F	G	H	I	J	K	L	M
1	●	●	●	●	●	●	●	●	●	●	●	●	●
2	●	●	●	●	●	●	●	●	●	●	●	●	●
3	●	●	●	●	●	●	●	●	●	●	●	●	●

A1-A3, C1-C3, E1-E3, F1-F3, G1-G3, H1-H2, I1-I3, J1-J3, L1-L3, C3-D3, E3-F3, A1-B1, E1-F1, G1-H1, G2-H3, J1-K2, L1-M3, K2-J3, A2-B2, G2-H2, L2-M2

ANCIENT STRUCTURES

STILL STANDING

Some ancient structures are still standing. There are pyramids around the world, but the most famous—the Great Pyramid of Giza—is in Egypt. It was built thousands of years ago. Another stone structure built thousands of years ago is southern England's Stonehenge. Scientists believe this massive stone circle could have been an observatory, a burial place, or a place of healing. No one knows for sure.

The Great Pyramid of Giza is the only structure listed as one of the Seven Wonders of the Ancient World that still stands.

17 PUZZLE ★★★★

Carved in Stone

Beginning at the top, work your way around to complete this design in one solid line, without picking up your pencil, retracing, or crossing over any line.

The largest vertical stones, at Stonehenge, called sarsen stones, were transported from 20 miles (32.2 km) away. Smaller bluestones came from Wales—a distance of 250 miles (402.3 km).

IN THE ARENA

The Colosseum in Rome, Italy, is a giant outdoor arena where gladiators fought. The Romans liked to watch animals fight each other, too. Nine thousand animals died in the first games there. What's most impressive about the Colosseum is that it was built without any of the machines and technology we use today. Think about it. No motorized cranes, trucks, or bulldozers!

The Roman Colosseum, built nearly 2,000 years ago, held as many as 50,000 spectators.

Splash!

Rome's Colosseum is so huge that its arena was sometimes flooded, so Roman spectators could watch ships engage in battle.

18 ★★★★ PUZZLE

Colosseum Count

These animals are all set to battle in the Colosseum. But being smart, the battle will be with numbers. Change each letter in an animal's name to match its number in the alphabet, with A as 1, B as 2, and so on. Add each number together to see who wins with the highest score. Can you predict who will win?

LION

ZEBRA

SNAKE

WOLF

FOLLOW THE LEADER

There are many different forms of government around the world. There are commonwealths, confederations, democracies, and dictatorships. Eighteen countries, including Jordan, Bhutan, Denmark, and Great Britain, have monarchies. That means each is ruled by a monarch—a king or queen. Other countries with royalty include the United Arab Emirates and the Sultanates of Oman and Brunei.

England's queen is Elizabeth II. She's reigned for almost 60 years.

Flying the Colors
Every country flies its flag as a unique symbol of its identity.

19 PUZZLE

Flag Fun

Can you identify the countries whose flags are shown here?

Sheikh Mohammed bin Rashid Al Maktoum is an emir—an Islamic prince—and the ruler of Dubai.

PUZZLE

Common Interests

What do Jamaica, Papua New Guinea, and New Zealand have in common?

To find out, fill in the blanks using the letters at the bottom of each column. The letters go in the spaces above them. We've done a couple for you, and for some boxes, there's only one possibility. Once you get a few, you should be able to get the rest.

Jamaica
This Caribbean island is the third largest English-speaking nation in the Western Hemisphere.

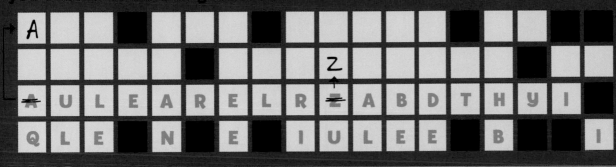

A

Z

A U L E A R E L R A B D T H Y I

Q L E N E I U L E E B I

AND TO THE REPUBLIC

The president is the head of the United States government, but there's another branch—the Congress—that also has a say in what laws are passed. In some monarchies, the king or queen is the leader of the country, but the everyday work of governing is done by other officials—often a prime minister or a parliament. That's what they have in Great Britain.

Britain's House of Parliament

Barack Obama became the first African-American President of the United States when he was sworn into office on January 20, 2009.

WHERE DO PEOPLE LIVE?

GIVE ME SOME ROOM!

Imagine 40 people living in your house! Wouldn't that be crowded? That's called population density—the number of people who live in a particular area. The more people there are per square mile or per square kilometer, the greater the population density. The population density of cities increases as more and more people move there looking for work.

Macau is part of the People's Republic of China. It's at the top of the list when it comes to population density. More than 541,200 people live there, on only 11.3 square miles (29.2 sq km) of land. That means that 47,894 people live on each square mile (18,534 per sq km). Now, that's crowded!

Crowds of people along a busy New York City street

Bangkok, Thailand
The population density of Bangkok, pictured here, is 10,435 people per square mile (4,029 per sq km).

21 PUZZLE

State The Problem

The part of the United States with the highest population density is the District of Columbia, but it's not a state. Use the clues to spell out the name of the U.S. state with the highest population density.

— — —   — — — — — — —

- The first letter appears in North, but not in South or District.
- The second, fifth, and eighth letters appear four times in Tennessee.
- The third letter begins Wisconsin and Wyoming.
- This state is the only one whose name contains this letter
- The sixth letter is the last letter in the name of Delaware's capital.
- The seventh letter appears only twice in Arkansas.
- The ninth letter appears at the end of Kentucky.

> ## Lots of Room
> Greenland is the world's largest island, but it has the lowest population density of any nation.

22 PUZZLE

Every Which Way

To find the name of the world's most densely populated sovereign nation, hold the book up to a mirror.

The answer to this puzzle is a tiny nation on the Mediterranean coast, surrounded on three sides by France. It is a popular tourist destination.

PEOPLE PLACES

Eleven of the world's cities each boast a population of over 8 million people, not including their surrounding suburbs. Seoul, South Korea, is the world's largest city, according to www.citymayors.com, with more than 10 million people. The others in this list are São Paulo, Brazil; Mumbai, India; Jakarta, Indonesia; Karachi, Pakistan; Moscow, Russia; Istanbul, Turkey; Mexico City, Mexico; Shanghai, China; and New York City, USA.

23 PUZZLE

On The Square

The letters A, B, I, L, R, and Z will fit in this grid in a unique pattern. Each letter will appear only once in each column, row, and group of six boxes. The name of the country where São Paulo is a major city will appear in one of the columns, reading from top to bottom.

	R				L
	Z	I			
I				A	
		L	R		
	L				
R				B	Z

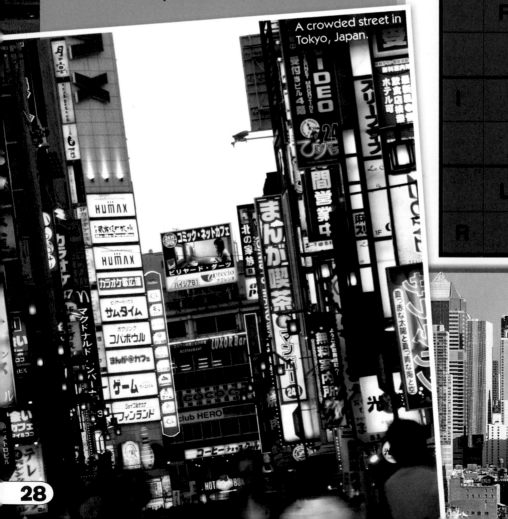

A crowded street in Tokyo, Japan.

24 PUZZLE

Population Squares

Populate each square of this puzzle with a line to connect the name of a country with its flag. No two lines can cross in any box, every box will have at least one line in it, and lines can only go horizontally or vertically, not diagonally.

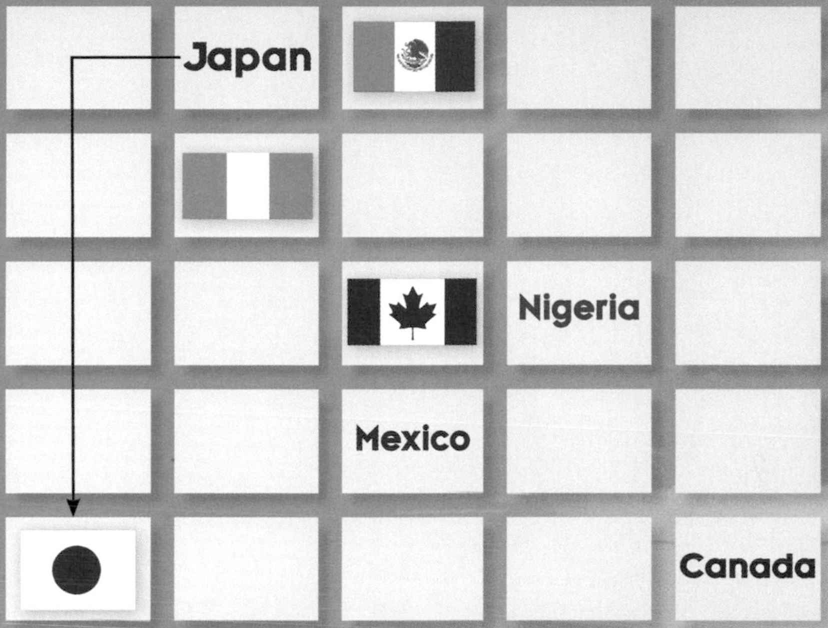

Japan
Nigeria
Mexico
Canada

The Pope's Home

Vatican City is the world's smallest independent nation, by area. It covers only 0.2 square miles (0.5 sq km).

SIZE WISE

Population isn't the only way to rank the size of a city. There's also land area. The U.S. city with more than 100,000 people that has the largest land area is Anchorage, Alaska. It covers 1,697 square miles (4,395.7 sq km). Jacksonville, Florida, is the next largest by area, followed by Oklahoma City, Oklahoma; Houston, Texas; and Phoenix, Arizona.

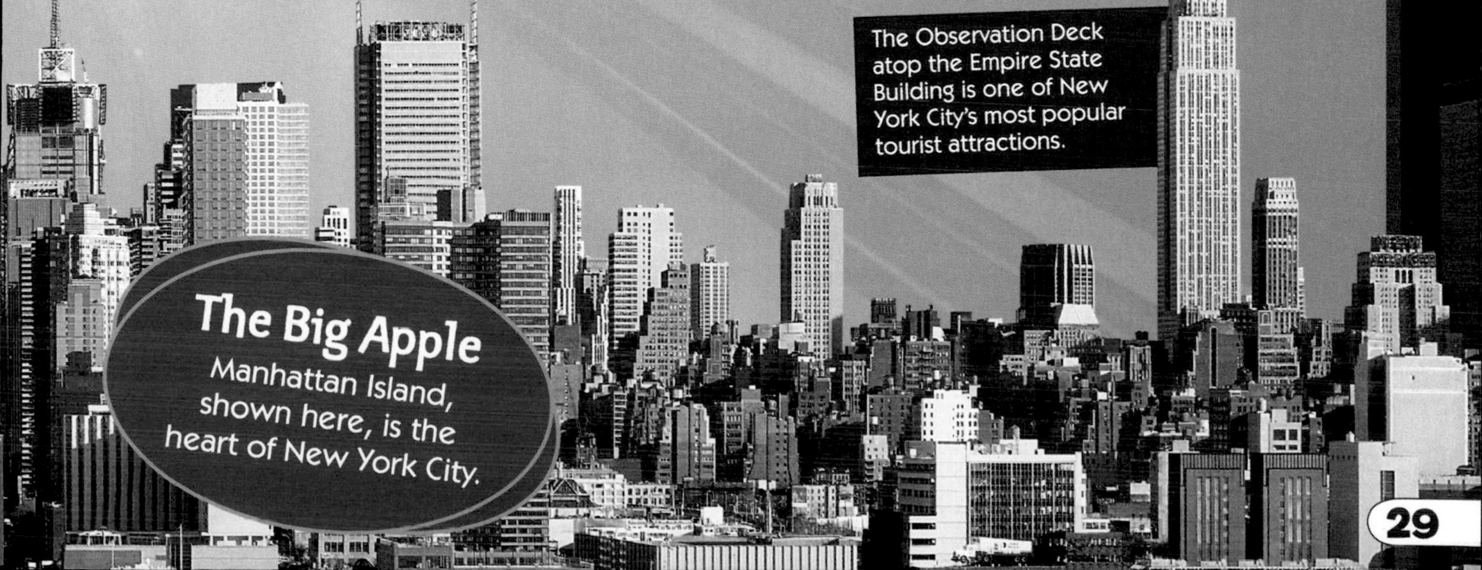

The Observation Deck atop the Empire State Building is one of New York City's most popular tourist attractions.

The Big Apple

Manhattan Island, shown here, is the heart of New York City.

POPULAR TOURIST DESTINATIONS

AWAY WE GO!

The world's cities offer fabulous attractions for you to see while on vacation. Paris, France, is the romantic "City of Light;" London, England, has a long history and charm; Tokyo, Japan, is a high-tech wonderland; and New York City, USA, is the cosmopolitan crossroads of the world.

Museums like the Louvre in Paris, the Museum of Modern Art in New York City, and the Prado in Madrid, Spain, are in large cities, but there are neat things to see outside large cities, too. Natural wonders such as the Grand Canyon, Niagara Falls, and the Rocky Mountains in North America, the outback of Australia, and the rain forests of Africa and South America are also great places to go.

The Airbus A380, shown here, is the largest passenger plane in the world, carrying more than 500 passengers.

Taj Mahal

The white-domed Taj Mahal, in Agra, India, was built between 1632 and 1653, as a tomb for the wife of Emperor Shah Jahan. Millions of people visit this site each year.

The Statue of Liberty, completed in 1886, stands on an island between New York City and New Jersey.

25 PUZZLE
★★★★★

Tourist Spots

Start on 1W, in the center of this puzzle, and follow the directions to eventually land at the beautiful Irish town of Dingle. You'll land on eight stops on your way. Each spot has both a direction (north, south, east, or west) to move and the number of spots to move. Bon voyage!

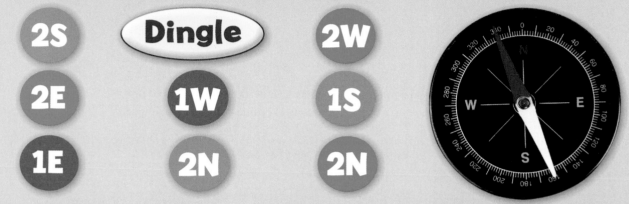

2S   Dingle   2W

2E   1W   1S

1E   2N   2N

26 PUZZLE
★★★★

A Capital Idea!

Connect each capital with its country. Draw a line from point to point through two letters. Write the letters in order from the first capital to the last to reveal the name of one of South America's tourist attractions.

Lima • E   S • Colombia
Quito • S   A • Brazil
Sucre • E   D • Venezuela
Bogotá • I   A • Peru
Brasilia • L   R • Bolivia
Caracas • N   T • Ecuador

_____
_____

THE ATMOSPHERE

UP IN THE AIR

The Earth's atmosphere helps protect life on Earth by warming the surface, by absorbing ultraviolet radiation from the sun, and by reducing the temperature differences between night and day. We live in the troposphere, the lowest level of the atmosphere.

Most of the water in the atmosphere is trapped in the troposphere, which helps make it the densest layer. The Karman Line, at an altitude of 62 miles (100 km) above the Earth, is the boundary between the atmosphere and space.

THERMOSPHERE 430 miles (690 km)

Space shuttle

MESOSPHERE 50 miles (80 km)

STRATOSPHERE 31 miles (50 km)

OZONE LAYER

TROPOSPHERE 7.5 miles (12 km)

Hot-air balloon

The ozone layer absorbs ultraviolet radiation and helps maintain the Earth's temperature.

TAKE A DEEP BREATH!

We don't breathe the same atmosphere as when the Earth was first formed, and thank goodness for that! Back then, it was mostly carbon dioxide and nitrogen. Those gases were released into the atmosphere from erupting volcanoes. Only when plants eventually developed and started taking in carbon dioxide and releasing oxygen did Earth's atmosphere become suitable for animal life.

27 PUZZLE
★★★☆☆

Gas Exchange

To find how plants are able to change carbon dioxide into oxygen, fill in each word clue. The highlighted letters will reveal the magic word.

A Hole in the Atmosphere

In 1985, scientists discovered a hole in the ozone layer above Antarctica, and determined it was caused by the gas used then in aerosol cans.

1. **A snapshot**
2. **The opposite of idle**
3. **Place after eighth**
4. **First book of the Old Testament:**

28 PUZZLE
★★★☆☆

Pie In The Sky

Can you identify which pie chart represents the Earth's current atmosphere? There's almost four times as much nitrogen as there is oxygen, but only 1/10th as much other gases as oxygen.

△ Hydrogen   △ Oxygen   △ Nitrogen

△ Water Vapor   △ Other Gases   △ Carbon Dioxide

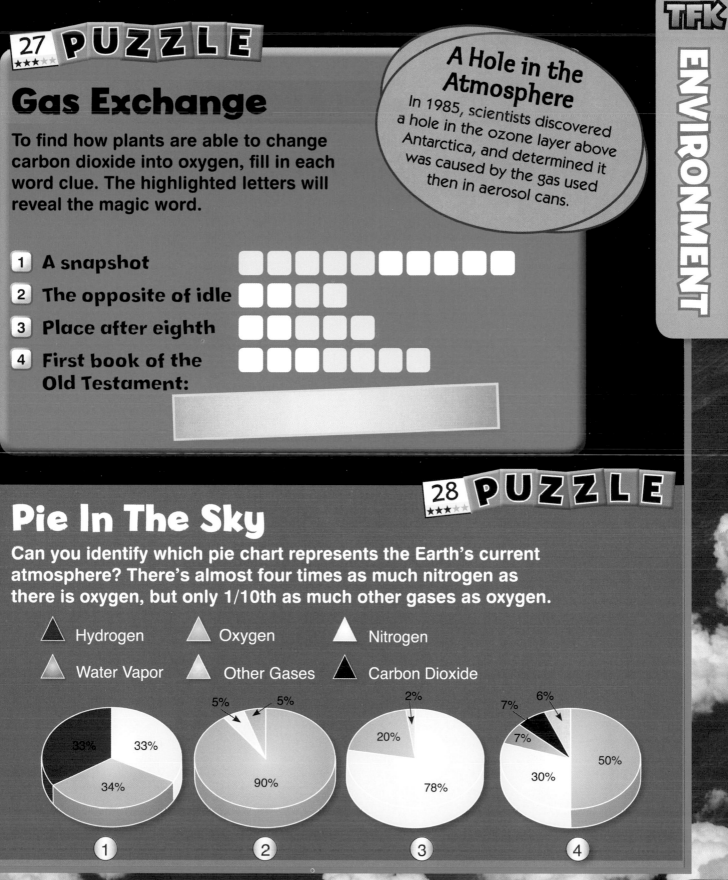

Chart 1: 33%, 33%, 34%

Chart 2: 5%, 5%, 90%

Chart 3: 2%, 20%, 78%

Chart 4: 6%, 7%, 7%, 50%, 30%

1   2   3   4

POLLUTION

THE CIRCLE OF LIFE

All the Earth's ecosystems are interconnected, so everything we do affects the environment. For example, when you fertilize your lawn, small bits of fertilizer can wash away into streams, rivers, or lakes. The fertilizer can pollute the water and cause plants in the water to grow bigger and faster than they naturally would have. This plant overgrowth can kill other plants, fish, other water animals, and mammals.

We need to **clean up** our act!

Other Kinds of Pollution

Did you know there are many kinds of pollution? There's noise pollution and light pollution, too. Too much of either one can harm plants, animals, and people.

29 PUZZLE
★★★★★

Can It!

Follow the directions to help put POLLUTION in its place.

- Write the word POLLUTION.   _____
- Change each O to an E.   _____
- Take the UTI and put it after the first L.   _____
- Change the T to a Y.   _____
- Change the P to an R.   _____
- Change every vowel except E to a C.   _____
- Remove the third letter and the last letter.   _____

A DIM VIEW

Global dimming happens when pollution and particles of soot and ash fill the air—like when a volcano erupts. This can prevent some of the sun's rays from reaching the Earth's surface, causing it to cool a little. It's what happened after Mount Pinatubo, in the Philippines, erupted in 1991. So much ash, dust, and smoke spewed into the air that the Earth stayed cooler for three years!

The ash, soot, and dust expelled by volcanoes are called particulates.

30 ★★★★ PUZZLE

Let the Sun Shine In

Global dimming results when too many particulates in the air don't allow the sun's rays to reach the Earth's surface. If you add each of the letters in S-U-N to the letters in each of the words below and then rearrange them, you should be able to form three brand new words.

S-U-N

IT   TAR   HIP

___ ___ ___ ___   ___ ___ ___ ___ ___ ___

___ ___ ___ ___ ___ ___

★HINT:
One of the new words is a planet!

Causing Famines?

Some scientists believe global dimming over the North Atlantic may have helped cause droughts in North Africa in the 1970s and 1980s, causing millions of people and animals to starve.

FOSSIL FUELS

PUT A DINOSAUR IN YOUR TANK

Fossil fuels are organic materials that come from the decomposed bodies of dinosaurs and early life-forms that have been squeezed in the Earth for millions of years, until they've turned to petroleum—oil and gas. Pools of oil and pockets of gas can be pumped out and used to make all sorts of products. Oil and gas won't last forever, though, so we need to come up with other fuel sources. And fast!

Fossils of dinosaurs like this one can be found in most natural history museums. Check 'em out!

31 PUZZLE

Rex Riddle

This riddle can be answered by the letters in the question. Each number in the answer indicates the placement of the letter in the question. (1=H, 2=O, 3=W, and so on).

How does every T-Rex communicate?

13-12-14-25-22-22-2-7-25-21-14-21-7   13-6-16-26

_____   _____

RENEWABLE ENERGY

POWER PROBLEMS

Alternative energy sources include nuclear, solar, water, and wind power. Fuels are also made from corn and sugar cane and even old food grease! Nuclear power has been in use since the 1950s, but the radioactive waste it produces is deadly to humans and other animals. Scientists are trying to come up with a better way to get rid of the waste, so nuclear power will be safer.

Nuclear power plants, like this one provide clean energy without creating air pollution.

Nuclear Power

Nuclear energy from fission powers electrical generating plants, ships and submarines, and creates nuclear isotopes used in medicine and industry.

32 PUZZLE
★☆☆☆☆

FISSION

The process of splitting atoms is called fission. It gives off a great deal of nuclear energy. Can you draw a line through this design that will split it in half, into mirror images of each other?

Today, wind farms like this one, with gigantic wind turbines, harvest energy from the wind.

TFK

THE OCEANS

Cruise ships carry people across the world's oceans.

WATER, WATER EVERYWHERE

About 70% of the world's surface is ocean, and oceans contain more than 95% of the planet's water. The Atlantic, Pacific, Indian, Arctic, and Great Southern Oceans are part of one huge body of water that circles the Earth. Some scientists estimate that there could be one million species of animals and plants living in the world's oceans.

Fun Fact

The Earth doesn't make new water molecules. Every drop that's on the Earth now has been here since the planet was formed.

33 PUZZLE
★★★★★

What's The Difference?

Can you spot the five differences between these two scenes?

Ocean Notion

A word relating to oceans can be found by choosing one letter from each group of three.

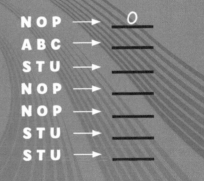

N O P → O
A B C → ___
S T U → ___
N O P → ___
N O P → ___
S T U → ___
S T U → ___

⭐

_ _ _ _ _ _ _

KEEPING CURRENT

Currents are like rivers within the oceans. They're caused by differences in temperature, salinity (saltiness), and wind. Ocean currents move all around the Earth in what's called the global conveyor belt. If a drop of water were carried all around the Earth on the global conveyor belt, scientists estimate it would take 1,000 years for it to return to where it started.

Sea turtles live in all the Earth's oceans except the Arctic. They can live up to 80 years.

Coral Reefs

Coral reefs in the world's oceans provide homes for hundreds of species of fish and other animals.

TALLEST MOUNTAINS

Did you know that rocks at the top of Mount Everest have fossils of marine animals in them? Cool, huh?

HIT THE HEIGHTS

Thirty of the world's highest mountains (measured from sea level) are in the Himalayas, a mountain range stretching 1,550 miles (2,500 km) across southern Asia. However, if we measured each mountain from its base to its tip, instead of from sea level, Mauna Kea, an inactive volcano in Hawaii, would be the world's tallest mountain. From the ocean floor to its peak, it's 6.3 miles (10.2 km).

35 PUZZLE

Re- Moving Mountains

The names of two North American mountains, one in South Dakota that has the faces of presidents on it, and one in northern California, have been brought together here. The letters appear in order but have been mixed together. Can you move the two mountains apart?

RSUSHHAMSTOREA

_ _ _ _ _ _ _

_ _ _ _ _ _

Growing Mountains

Huge sections of the Earth's crust—called tectonic plates—are very gradually colliding with each other, causing mountains to be formed. In fact, the mountains in the Himalayas are constantly getting taller!

TOP OF THE WORLD

The highest mountain on Earth is Mount Everest, in the Himalayas. It measures an impressive 5.5 miles (8.9 km) above sea level. Aconcagua, in Argentina, is South America's highest peak, measuring 4.3 miles (6.9 km). It's part of the Andes mountain range, and the world's highest mountain outside Asia. The highest mountain in the United States is Alaska's Mount McKinley. It comes in at 3.85 miles (6.2 km).

Aconcagua can be dangerous. The "White Wind," clouds that descend its upper slopes, can trap climbers.

Andes

The longest mountain range on the surface of the Earth is the Andes. It stretches more than 5,000 miles (8,046.7 km) along the west side of South America.

36 PUZZLE ★★★★

Guided Tour

There is a group of people from Nepal who act as guides for anyone trying to climb Mount Everest. Use the clues to find out what these guides are called.

The first letter appears in both summit and scale. _____

The second letter appears at the beginning of both hike and helper. _____

The third letter appears in Rainier, but not in rain. _____

The fourth letter appears at both ends of Rainier. _____

The fifth letter appears in Alps, but not in landslide. _____

The sixth letter appears in Alps, but not in plus. _____

_ _ _ _ _ _

TFK
LONGEST RIVERS

The Nile flows northward through Egypt into the Mediterranean Sea.

A RIVER RUNS

Each of the world's four longest rivers is on a different continent. The Nile in Africa is the longest, at 4,132 miles (6,654 km). The Amazon crosses South America for 3,980 miles (6,405 km). The Yangtze travels 3,915 miles (6,300 km) through China, and the Mississippi and Missouri rivers combine for a total of 3,870 miles (6,228 km) through the United States, qualifying as North America's longest river.

Mighty Mississippi

Did you know that the Mississippi River actually begins in northern Minnesota, at Lake Itasca?

37 PUZZLE
★★★☆☆

Half Time

Henry Hudson was a famous explorer. There's a river in New York named after him. To find the name of Henry Hudson's ship, consider the letters below:

_____ _____ _____ _____

RIVER RETURNS

Rivers provide lots of recreation—sailing, fishing, scuba diving, canoeing, water skiing, rafting, tubing, and more. They're also an important ecosystem for plants and animals, providing places for fish to spawn and thrive.

The force of a river can provide power for hydro-electric dams to generate electricity. Goods and people are transported down rivers from one city to another. Are you thirsty? Rivers are major suppliers of drinking water, so we'd better protect them and keep them clean.

Whitewater
Some rivers flow downhill very quickly, creating rapids and waterfalls. People enjoy the thrill of riding those rapids in inflatable boats.

Whitewater rafting can be quite dangerous, so always raft with an expert.

The force of rivers like this one in northern Canada can carve rocks into interesting shapes.

38 PUZZLE
★★★★★

Ride The Rivers

As you ride the river down, remove one letter at each level. Rearrange the remaining letters to form a common word. Strong rafters will be able to go all the way down to a single-letter word.

R I V E R S

◆ Something you stand on in choir class   __ __ __ __ __

◆ Title for a king   __ __ __ __

◆ Title of respect used often in the army   __ __ __

◆ Simple present-tense verb, as in: This _ _ my book   __ __

◆ Pronoun for yourself   __

DESERTS

HOW DRY I AM

Deserts are dry regions that receive less than 10 inches (25.4 cm) of rain per year. The most common type of desert is the tradewind desert. The Sahara, in northern Africa, is a tradewind desert. The driest desert in the world, though, is the Atacama, on the western coast of South America. As many as 20 years may pass in the Atacama without any measurable rainfall.

Mojave
The Mojave Desert, in southern California and Nevada, western Arizona, and the southwestern corner of Utah, is the hottest desert in North America.

These sand dunes, in Death Valley, California, are formed by wind pushing the sand around.

39 PUZZLE
★★☆☆☆

Word Play

Follow these instructions.

1. Write down the subject of these two pages. _____

2. Now double one letter to find something sweet. _____

3. Now write the word backward to show how you sometimes feel before taking a big test. _____

PUZZLE

Back Code

To solve this riddle, go back one letter in the alphabet.

Why don't travelers get hungry in the desert?

Cfdbvtf pg uif tboe xijdi jt uifsf.

_____

THE BIG SANDY

Talk about your big sandboxes! There are deserts on every continent. South America has the Atacama Desert, Australia the Great Sandy, and the U.S. the Mojave. Antarctica, even though it's not hot and sandy, is still a desert, because it receives little rain. In fact, it's the world's largest desert, covering more than 5.5 million square miles (14.2 million sq km). The world's largest sand desert is the Sahara in Africa, which covers 3.5 million square miles (9.1 million sq km).

Death Valley

Death Valley—part of the Mojave Desert—has the hottest, driest, and lowest points in the United States.

LARGEST LAKES

LOTSA WATER, BUT IS IT A LAKE?

A lake is a body of water of considerable size and depth that's surrounded by land and fed by rivers or streams. The Caspian Sea, just north of Iran, fits that description, but it's not called a lake. It's called a sea. That's probably because it contains salt water. Does that mean it's the world's largest lake or one of the world's smallest seas?

Loch Means Lake

Loch Ness is a famous lake in Scotland. (Loch is the Scottish word for lake.) Loch Ness is supposed to be home to an amazing creature—Nessie, the Loch Ness Monster!

41 PUZZLE
★★★☆☆

Picture Puzzle

What saying or phrase is represented in this picture?

sailing

CCCCCCC

GREAT BIG LAKES!

Lake Superior is the largest freshwater lake in the world. It covers 31,820 square miles (82,414 sq km). Two other Great Lakes—Huron and Michigan—are also on the list of the world's 10 biggest freshwater lakes. It's estimated that the five Great Lakes together hold about one fifth of the world's supply of fresh water.

The north shore of Lake Superior, seen here, is a great place to fish, water ski, hike, camp, and swim, but watch out! The water's pretty cold, even in summer.

Lotsa Lakes

Approximately 60% of the world's lakes are in Canada.

If you were standing on the moon, you could see the Great Lakes, and you'd recognize the familiar wolf-head shape of Lake Superior.

42 PUZZLE ★★☆☆☆

That's Great!

The word HOMES contains the first letter of the names of each of the Great Lakes. Can you name them?

H _____

O _____

M _____

E _____

S _____

TFK RAIN FORESTS

Some animals live on the floors of rain forests, others live on tree trunks and branches, and still others live high in the canopies of the trees.

TREE TYPES

Tropical rain forests are near the Equator, where it's really hot and steamy! Jungles are the densest sections of tropical rain forests—full of wildlife, tall trees, sweltering temperatures, and swing-able vines. You know—Tarzan's playground! South America, Africa, and Southeast Asia all have tropical rain forests.

43 PUZZLE
★★★★★

Common Bonds

What do trees have in common with each of the following?

1. **Main libraries** sometimes have smaller ones called _____
2. **Another name for a book's pages** _____
3. **Dogs talk to each other when they** _____
4. **The noses on elephants are called** _____

What A Waste!

It's estimated that 30 acres (12.14 hec) of rain forest are cut down or destroyed every minute.

IMPORTANT LINKS

Rain forests are home to nearly 90% of the world's species of plants and animals. Rain forests are a vital source of materials used to make medicines, too! Pharmaceutical companies—the ones who create medicines—experiment with all kinds of plants, looking for drugs that can fight or cure diseases like cancer. They study leaves, branches, petals, and roots of rain forest plants, hoping for the next wonder cure.

44 PUZZLE

★★★★★

★HINT:
In some cases, ignore the punctuation.

Hidden Trees

Find the name of a tree hidden in each sentence. The letters of the tree name appear in order and unscrambled, but they're spread between two or more words.

1 "Hand me the map, Leroy."   _ _ _ _ _

2 "Hey, pal, my brother expected
   you here by noon," Tim said.   _ _ _ _

3 "We've been waiting out here
   since dark."   _ _ _ _ _

4 "I want to sleep in Edward's bed." _ _ _ _ _

THE ARCTIC

Seals sun themselves on an ice floe in the Arctic Ocean.

Polar bears are in danger of extinction, because the ice sheets on which they live are melting, making it harder for them to find food.

A SEA OF ICE

Looking down at the North Pole from space, the sea ice that covers the Arctic is a bright, white blanket. Unlike the ice at the South Pole, though, there isn't a landmass underneath this ice. It's floating over the Arctic Ocean. The sea ice in the Arctic is home to polar bears, seals, and Arctic terns.

45 PUZZLE

Word Swap

To change ICE to CAP, change one letter to create a new word at each step.

ICE

_ _ _   The highest card

_ _ _   Take part in a movie or play

_ _ _   Prone to (It rhymes with napped)

_ _ _   Choose (It's part of "option")

_ _ _   Grain for cereal

_ _ _   A feline

CAP

ANTARCTICA

THE BOTTOM OF THE WORLD

With a landmass of 5.4 million square miles (13.98 million sq km), Antarctica is the world's largest continent. Huge mountains and massive ice sheets cover most of the land. Do you know how cold it is in Antarctica? Temperatures can reach a bone-chilling -128.6° F (-88° C). Antarctica is a land of ice, but only two inches (5.1 cm) of snow fall each year. Penguins and other animals live near the coast of Antarctica, but never venture more than 60 miles (96.6 km) inland. The climate away from the coast is just too harsh.

Ice Anyone?
Antarctica contains about 87% of the world's ice.

46 ★★★★ PUZZLE

Isn't That Ice?

All the words that fill in this puzzle go nice with ICE. For example, an answer might be (ice) BUCKET or (ice) BOX. When you fill in all the words correctly, read down the blue column to find an important temperature scale scientists use.

1. How to hook something in winter — ICE ▢▢▢▢
2. Manny, Sid, and Diego lived then — ICE ▢▢▢
3. Rangers and Bruins play this — ICE ▢▢▢▢▢
4. Frozen dessert — ICE ▢▢▢▢
5. Huge ice that sank the *Titanic* — ICE ▢▢▢▢
6. Place to play #3 or do #10 — ICE ▢
7. Container for icing down sodas — ICE ▢▢▢▢
8. A small block of ice — ICE ▢▢▢
9. A small tool for chipping — ICE ▢▢▢
10. To glide across ice, wear this — ICE ▢▢▢▢

Emperor penguins are the largest penguins, standing about 45 inches (115 cm) tall. These flightless birds live in Antarctica.

51

TFK FAMOUS SCIENTISTS

GREAT THINKERS

Gregor Mendel was an Austrian monk whose work with pea plants formed the basis for the study of genetics. Louis Pasteur, a French chemist and biologist, discovered that diseases are spread by living organisms called microbes.

French scientist Marie Curie discovered the element radium and found a way to measure radioactive materials. German-born Albert Einstein developed the Theory of Relativity ($E=MC^2$), that basically states that a very small amount of matter—like an atom—can release a large amount of energy.

Louis Pasteur proved that certain diseases can be prevented by immunizations—by getting shots that keep the diseases from happening.

English scientist Sir Isaac Newton was one of the greatest scientists of all time. Here, he is studying the properties of light.

47 PUZZLE
★★★☆☆

Sign Out

This digital display should show the name of an important scientist, but some of the lights are burned out. For each letter of his name, one "light" that's supposed to be lit isn't. Also, if a letter is repeated, the burned out part will be the same each time. Can you fill in the gaps to spell his name?

The scientist whose name appears above invented the astronomical telescope and used it to study the moon, the planets, and the stars.

INVENTORS AND THEIR INVENTIONS

48 PUZZLE
★★★★★

First Things First

Take the first letter from each item pictured to spell out the name of the famous inventor pictured below.

- - - - - -
- - - - -

BRIGHT IDEAS

Ever go for a walk and get burrs stuck to your clothes? That's what happened to Swiss inventor George de Mestral. He looked at the burrs under a microscope and saw tiny hooks on the seed that gripped the cloth. This led him to invent Velcro.

Let's not forget two famous American inventors—Benjamin Franklin and Thomas Edison. Franklin, one of America's founding fathers, invented bifocal eyeglasses, the lightning rod, the Franklin stove, and the odometer. Edison invented hundreds of things, including the light bulb, phonograph, and motion-picture camera.

Benjamin Franklin, shown here, was more than an inventor. He was also a diplomat, statesman, printer, and author.

GREAT DISCOVERIES

OUTSIDE THE BOX

Great discoveries often dispute accepted theories. Galileo, the "Father of Modern Science," used his telescope and mathematics to prove that the Earth revolves around the sun, and not the other way around. American Robert Ballard discovered that there is life in the very deepest parts of the ocean, near vents on the ocean floor that spew out volcanic gases.

Galileo built the first high-powered telescope and unlocked many of the secrets of astronomy.

ALVIN, the deep-sea submarine used by Robert Ballard to observe life on the ocean floor

49 PUZZLE

Number, Number

Can you "discover" a four-digit number? Adding these four digits equals 24. The first digit is one third of the second digit, and the third digit is two more than the fourth digit, which itself is two more than the first. All the digits are different, single numbers.

Fun Fact

Liquid Paper, that white stuff you use to correct your written mistakes, was invented by Mike Nesmith's mom. Mike was one of the Monkees, a pop singing group back in the 1960s.

Measure Of Success

Accidents?
Potato chips, artificial sweeteners, microwave ovens, Post-it Notes, the Slinky, corn flakes, and Silly Putty are just a few of the inventions people have come up with accidentally, while trying to create something else.

Use the measurements beneath each space to spell out the germ-fighting medicine Alexander Fleming discovered accidentally because he didn't clean his lab.

0	1	2	3	4	5	6
	C	L	I	P	E	N

___ ___ ___ ___ ___ ___ ___ ___ ___ ___
4" 5" 6" 3" 1" 3" 2" 2" 3" 6"

ACCIDENTALLY ON PURPOSE

Some of the greatest scientific discoveries have happened by accident. Wilhelm Roentgen discovered X-rays while working on another experiment. Anton Van Leeuwenhoek was making lenses for microscopes when he accidentally discovered microorganisms in a droplet of water. The greatest accidental discoverer was Christopher Columbus. He bumped into the Americas when he thought he was on his way to India!

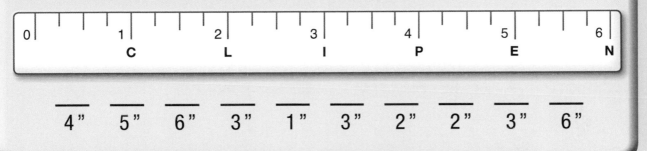

Christopher Columbus, who first made landfall in the Americas somewhere in the Bahamas, always believed he had reached Asia.

All Time TOP MOVIES

Robert Pattinson and Kristen Stewart, from *The Twilight Saga: New Moon.*

OFF TO A GOOD START

The Twilight Saga: New Moon broke the U.S. box office record for a single day, earning $72.7 million. The previous record was held by *The Dark Knight*, which premiered in 2008 and earned $67.2 million. *Avatar*, the 2009 futuristic blockbuster, didn't break the one-day box office record, but it has become the world-wide top money-making film of all time.

Christian Bale and Heath Ledger, as Batman and The Joker.

51 PUZZLE

Playing Parts

Can you name the actor pictured below who starred in, or provided the voice of, one of the characters in each of these four movies?

1 *Astro Boy*

2 *August Rush*

3 *The Spiderwick Chronicles*

4 *The Golden Compass*

_ _ _ _ _ _ _ _ _

Movies and Television

Box Office

Find these "box" words.

- **Prizefighter** _____

- **Part of a train** _____

- **Old-fashioned refrigerator** _____

- **Machine that plays music when you put in a coin** _____

- **Place for hammers or wrenches** _____

Life in the forests of the moon Pandora is anything but ordinary for the characters of *Avatar*.

THE BIG SHOW

It's named after a disaster, yet *Titanic* was anything but! This movie was the world's top money-making film of all time, having earned $1.84 billion, at least until *Avatar* came along. *Avatar* is expected to earn more than $2 billion. *Lord of the Rings: Return of the King* stands in third place at $1.12 billion.

Fun Fact
The Lord of the Rings movies were filmed in New Zealand, near a place called Matamata.

ANIMATION

PICTURE PERFECT

Since 1914, when Gertie the dinosaur walked around in one of the very first animated films, kids and adults have loved cartoons. A talking car may seem ridiculous, but with help from skilled animators and storytellers, the car comes to life. From animals in the forest to toys on the shelf to monsters under the bed, animation brings movement and life to even the wildest creatures.

B.O.B., from
Monsters vs. Aliens

53 ★★★★☆ PUZZLE

Common Bond

Can you name the actor pictured below who provided the voices of these animated characters from *Toy Story*, *Ratatouille*, and *Cars*?

2 2A 32 ISO 80 32 32B

_____ _____

_____

★PUZZLE★

Who's hiding?

Fill in these blanks about animated films, and then read the first letters, from top to bottom, to reveal the lead character from a famous Disney animated film.

- Pooh and Boog are: ___ ___ ___ ___ ___

- Master of Pikachu: ___ ___ ___

- _____Vs. Aliens: ___ ___ ___ ___ ___ ___ ___ ___

- Sponge with square pants: ___ ___ ___

- Age when Manny, Sid, and Diego lived: ___ ___ ___

STOP AND GO

Stop-action animation requires thousands of tiny movements of models and figures to make them seem to come to life. The master of stop-action animation was Ray Harryhausen. His films include *Mighty Joe Young* and *Jason and the Argonauts*. Harryhausen was inspired by Willis O'Brien, who did the animation for the first King Kong movie in 1933. More recent films using stop-action animation are *The Nightmare Before Christmas*, *Chicken Run*, and *Fantastic Mr. Fox*.

All in a Word

To animate, according to the dictionary, is to give life. Animators certainly seem to do that!

Mr. Fox promised his wife Felicity that he wouldn't raid farms anymore to steal chickens, but he and his friends decide one more raid wouldn't hurt, in the 2009 stop-action animated film *Fantastic Mr. Fox*.

SUPER HEROES

55 ★★★☆☆ PUZZLE

Alter Egos

Can you name the superheroes who used the following alter egos?

- **Peter Parker** _____
- **Scott Summers** _____
- **Clark Kent** _____
- **Bruce Wayne** _____
- **Dr. Bruce Banner** _____

The Man of Steel

Did you know that Superman first appeared in Action Comics #1, which came out in June 1938? Guess that makes the Man of Steel more than 70 years old!

POW!

Many modern blockbuster movies feature characters that were first famous in comic books. Batman, Superman, Spider-Man, Doc Savage, Dick Tracy, Daredevil, and the Hulk have all starred in movies. The X-Men were a group of mutants in comics before starring in a series of films. Wolverine has become a hero everyone loves, and that's funny, because it's the last thing he'd want!

Wolverine, played by Hugh Jackman, fights for the rights of mutants in the *X-Men* movies, but shuns the spotlight.

George Reeves and Phyllis Coates starred in the 1950s TV series, *Adventures of Superman*.

PUZZLE
★★☆☆☆

City Scene

Match the superhero with the city he patrols:

Batman ●   ● Central City

Superman ●   ● New York City

Spider-Man ●   ● Gotham City

The Flash ●   ● Metropolis

BAM!

Adam West and Burt Ward—TV's Dynamic Duo.

Some comic book superheroes were on TV before they were in movies. Superman was one of the first TV superheroes, back when TV was black and white. Batman—the Caped Crusader—had his own show during the 1960s. It was on two nights in a row each week, with a cliffhanger at the end of the first episode to get you to watch the second night.

To the Bat Cave!
Viewers of the TV series *Batman* in the 1960s loved all the gadgets Batman and Robin used to fight crime.

TFK ROCK STARS

Rock and Roll includes many different types of music, from Pop to Acid to Metal to Country Rock. To publicize their work, performers often go on tour when a new CD is released. The #1 money-earning rock band in the world is the Rolling Stones, who earned more than $88 million in just 15 months. Other top-earning bands include U2, Bon Jovi, the Black Eyed Peas, and the Beatles. No artists have had more impact on music than the Beatles, the Rolling Stones, and Elvis Presley. The Rock and Roll Hall of Fame's "500 Songs that Shaped Rock and Roll" lists seven Beatles tunes, and six each for the Stones and Elvis.

57 PUZZLE
★★★★

Top Sellers
An album is certified platinum by the Recording Industry Association of America (RIAA) for sales over one million copies.

Chart Toppers

Can you match these *Billboard* top-10 rock albums with the groups that recorded them?

Contra ●	● Owl City
Dark Horse ●	● Kings of Leon
Leave this Town ●	● Vampire Weekend
Ocean Eyes ●	● Spoon
Transference ●	● Daughtry
Only by the Night ●	● Nickelback

DIVINE DIVAS PUZZLE

Diva Diversion

Unscramble the letters of these four common words to discover the name of the actress and singer who stars in the *High School Musical* movies.

sends - hug - vane - as

Miley is a shortened version of Smiley, because when she was a baby, she smiled all the time.

Mary J. Blige, the Queen of Hip Hop Soul

DIVINE DIVAS

Divas are female singers who command the stage with their presence and voice. Aretha Franklin, the "Queen of Soul," certainly qualifies. She was declared #1 on *Rolling Stone's* list of all-time greatest singers. Barbra Streisand's the only artist to win #1 Album awards in five separate decades. Diana Ross, a true diva, helped establish the Motown sound in the 1960s. Modern divas have included Miley Cyrus, Kelly Clarkson, Mary J. Blige, Leona Lewis, Jennifer Hudson, and country singer Martina McBride.

A Worthy Cause

The Save the Music Foundation, sponsored by VH1, has raised more than $25 million to buy musical instruments for schools.

FEEL THE BEAT

JAZZ IS JAZZ

Louis Armstrong said, "If you have to ask for a definition of jazz, you'll never know what jazz is." Jazz musicians sort of make it up as they go along. One jazz giant was Charlie "Bird" Parker. Another was John Coltrane. Miles Davis, a jazz trumpeter, invented cool jazz—West Coast Jazz—known for its mellow sounds. Cool, Man, Cool!

Miles Davis was one of the most influential jazz musicians of all time, with a career that spanned 50 years.

59 ★★☆☆☆ PUZZLE

'ake A Note

Musical notation depends on the placement of notes on a scale. A small scale is shown here. The name of a leafy vegetable is spelled out using only musical notes. Can you tell what it is?

All That Jazz!
Jazz, a purely American style of music, had its origins about 100 years ago in New Orleans, Louisiana. Today, there are jazz festivals across the country. Check 'em out!

F
E
D
C
B
A
G
F
E

Hip hop is an outgrowth of rap. Jay-Z is one its most successful stars, having sold over 30 million albums. Diddy is another hip hop artist who's taken his success beyond the music scene, influencing fashion, movies, and art.

Many rap and hip hop artists have been involved in highly-publicized feuds. TuPac Shakur and Notorious B.I.G. are two who died violently, mirroring the violent lyrics of many early rap and hip hop songs.

Rapper and hip hop star Jay-Z does more than sing. He also owns the Nets, an NBA team. Guess that makes them the New Jay-Z Nets, huh?

60 PUZZLE
★★★★★

Hip Hop To It

Hop from box to box to spell out the name of Jay-Z's record company. All letters are used once.

★HINT: The answer is similar to the New York City setting for the TV series *30 Rock*.

A
L
L E
   F
C A
   O
R

START

Formerly Known As

Hip Hop music was originally known as "disco rap."

Sean Combs, pictured here, was first known as Puff Daddy, then P. Diddy. Now, he's just Diddy in the U.S.

HOME RUN KINGS

On August 8, 2007, Barry Bonds of the San Francisco Giants belted a home run over the right field wall at AT&T Park. Although Bonds had hit hundreds of home runs before, this one was special. It was home run #756, and with it, he broke the all-time home run record of 755, set by Hank Aaron in 1974. Bonds would hit six more homers during the season, for a total of 762.

Hammerin' Hank Aaron

Barry Bonds hits his historic 756th home run in 2007. A fan later paid $750,000 for that baseball.

61 PUZZLE

Home Run Hitters as of the 2009 season	
Barry Bonds	762
Hank Aaron	755
Babe Ruth	714
Willie Mays	660
Ken Griffey Jr.	630
Sammy Sosa	609
Frank Robinson	586
Mark McGwire	583
Alex Rodriguez	583
Harmon Killebrew	573
Rafael Palmeiro	569

Batter Up!

Besides being in the top 11 all-time home run champs, four of these sluggers have something in common that the other seven don't share. Using the chart of Home Run Hitters, write the last name of each record holder on the lines next to the matching number of home runs. When the names are filled in, put the numbered letters into the proper spaces to reveal the common element.

569 → _ _ _ _ _ _ _
        2 4

630 → _ _ _ _ _ _ _
            6   5 7

762 → _ _ _ _ _
        1

714 → _ _ _ _
          3

They each
_ _ _   _ _ _ _
1 2 3   4 5 6 3 7

62 PUZZLE

★★★★★

Slam Dunk

When each of the words in the Word Box is written in the grid, from left to right, another word will be revealed extending down the left column. The size of each word is a clue to where it belongs. Getting them all correct is a slam dunk!

WORD BOX: alley-oop, assist, backboard, block, elbow, key, layup, line, shot, turnover

Shaquille O'Neal was named one of the top NBA players of all time in 1996. His first name means "little warrior" in Arabic.

Blazing The Trail

In 1950, Nat "Sweetwater" Clifton became the first African-American player to sign a contract with an NBA team, the New York Knickerbockers.

IN THE NBA

There are currently 29 professional teams in the National Basketball Association (NBA). California has four, the most of any state. The Boston Celtics have won the NBA championship 18 times, more than any other team. Basketball was officially introduced as an Olympic sport in the 1936 Games. Since that time, the United States team has won a majority of these gold medals.

TFK AN UPSETTING SUPER BOWL

The New England Patriots were almost perfect. They'd gone the entire regular 2007 football season without a loss. The New York Giants, however, defeated the "perfect" Patriots 17-14 in Super Bowl XLII—in one of the greatest upsets in Super Bowl history.

Eli Manning

Tom Brady

David Tyree catches a pass as New England Patriots safety Rodney Harrison tries to break up the play in the fourth quarter.

63 PUZZLE
★★★★

Wins—Losses

With their win in the 2008 Super Bowl, the Giants tied the Patriots for the most Super Bowl wins. Which of these two teams has lost the most Super Bowls? To figure it out, follow each set of clues:

	1st Q	2nd Q	3rd Q	4th Q	Final
Giants	3	0	0	14	17
Patriots	0	7	0	7	14

For the Patriots

Divide Tom Brady's number by the number of points in a touchdown. Add the number of points scored on a successful Point After Touchdown to find the number of Super Bowl losses for the Patriots.

For the Giants

Multiply the number of points scored by the Giants in the first quarter of Super Bowl XLII by the number of quarters in a standard regulation game. Subtract Eli Manning's number. Subtract the number of quarters in which no team scored during this Super Bowl to get the number of Super Bowl losses for the Giants.

68

OLYMPICS

The Summer Olympics feature short-distance and long-distance races, like this one.

PUZZLE

A Weighty Question

You'll win the gold if you can figure out the weight of each medal and how many bronze medals need to be on the final scale.

Gold   Silver   Bronze

Athletes from around the world met in Beijing, China, for the 2008 Summer Olympics.

FOR THE RECORD

Russian gymnast Larysa Latynina has the most Olympic medals of any athlete—18. American swimmer Michael Phelps holds the record for the most gold medals—8—in a single year. Eddie Eagan of the United States is the only person to have won a gold medal in both the Summer (boxing) and Winter (bobsledding) Games. Swedish sharpshooter Oscar Swahn, at almost 73 years of age, is the oldest person to earn a medal.

Special Games
The Paralympics, Special Olympics, and Youth Olympics are other international competitions.

69

STATE NICKNAMES

ALOHA, STATE!

Do you have a nickname? Every U.S. state has one. Texas is the "Lone Star State," and New Jersey is the "Garden State." Missouri is the "Show Me State," and Hawaii is the "Aloha State." (Aloha is Hawaiian for love, but mostly, it's used to say hello.)

States can be nicknamed for most anything. Georgia is the "Peach State," Louisiana is the "Pelican State," Connecticut is the "Constitution State," and Arizona is the "Grand Canyon State." Alaska is called "The Last Frontier" and "Land of the Midnight Sun." During the summer, it's daylight all night long in parts of Alaska!

65 PUZZLE

"Come in, Dear!"

Each state in the U.S. has a two-letter postal abbreviation. Can you identify the states whose postal abbreviations appear in the title of this puzzle? Each abbreviation is complete and in its proper order.

CA   MO   NY

For a list of states, capitals, and postal abbreviations, see page 71.

Which Came First?

Did you know New York's state nickname is the Empire State? Now, was the building named after the state or the state after the building?

The Lower 48

WA MT ND MN
ID SD
WY
NV UT NE IA NY
CA CO OK MO VA
AZ NM NC
TX LA NC

"Big" Cities

Many U.S. cities have nicknames, too. Cities in New York, Louisiana, Hawaii, Georgia, and Oklahoma each have the word "Big" in their nicknames. Can you identify all five?

1. The Big Apple: _____

2. The Big Easy: _____

3. The Big Pineapple: _____

4. The Big Peach: _____

5. The Big Friendly: _____

U. S. States, Capitals, and Postal Abbreviations

State (Capital)	Abbr.
ALABAMA (Montgomery)	AL
ALASKA (Juneau)	AK
ARIZONA (Phoenix)	AZ
ARKANSAS (Little Rock)	AR
CALIFORNIA (Sacramento)	CA
COLORADO (Denver)	CO
CONNECTICUT (Hartford)	CT
DELAWARE (Dover)	DE
FLORIDA (Tallahassee)	FL
GEORGIA (Atlanta)	GA
HAWAII (Honolulu)	HI
IDAHO (Boise)	ID
ILLINOIS (Springfield)	IL
INDIANA (Indianapolis)	IN
IOWA (Des Moines)	IA
KANSAS (Topeka)	KS
KENTUCKY (Frankfort)	KY
LOUISIANA (Baton Rouge)	LA
MAINE (Augusta)	ME
MARYLAND (Annapolis)	MD
MASSACHUSETTS (Boston)	MA
MICHIGAN (Lansing)	MI
MINNESOTA (St. Paul)	MN
MISSISSIPPI (Jackson)	MS
MISSOURI (Jefferson City)	MO
MONTANA (Helena)	MT
NEBRASKA (Lincoln)	NE
NEVADA (Carson City)	NV
NEW HAMPSHIRE (Concord)	NH
NEW JERSEY (Trenton)	NJ
NEW MEXICO (Santa Fe)	NM
NEW YORK (Albany)	NY
NORTH CAROLINA (Raleigh)	NC
NORTH DAKOTA (Bismarck)	ND
OHIO (Columbus)	OH
OKLAHOMA (Oklahoma City)	OK
OREGON (Salem)	OR
PENNSYLVANIA (Harrisburg)	PA
RHODE ISLAND (Providence)	RI
SOUTH CAROLINA (Columbia)	SC
SOUTH DAKOTA (Pierre)	SD
TENNESSEE (Nashville)	TN
TEXAS (Austin)	TX
UTAH (Salt Lake City)	UT
VERMONT (Montpelier)	VT
VIRGINIA (Richmond)	VA
WASHINGTON (Olympia)	WA
WEST VIRGINIA (Charleston)	WV
WISCONSIN (Madison)	WI
WYOMING (Cheyenne)	WY

STATE CAPITALS

FOREIGN INFLUENCE

America is a nation of different cultures. Many early cultural influences can still be seen in the names of our state capitals. Some remnants of America's French roots exist in such capital names as Des Moines, Pierre, Montpelier, Cheyenne, Boise, and Baton Rouge. Spanish influenced the names of Santa Fe and Sacramento.

There's Greek influence in Olympia, Phoenix, and Helena. Germans contributed Bismarck and Frankfort. Native Americans named Topeka, Little Rock, and Honolulu.

67 PUZZLE
★★★★★

You Know This

D'you know the name of Alaska's capital? Of course you do! Just add the sixth month of the year to the chemical symbol for gold. D'you know it now?

What's in a Name?
Des Moines is French for "monks" or "of the monks." Trappist monks once lived in huts above the river near this Iowa city.

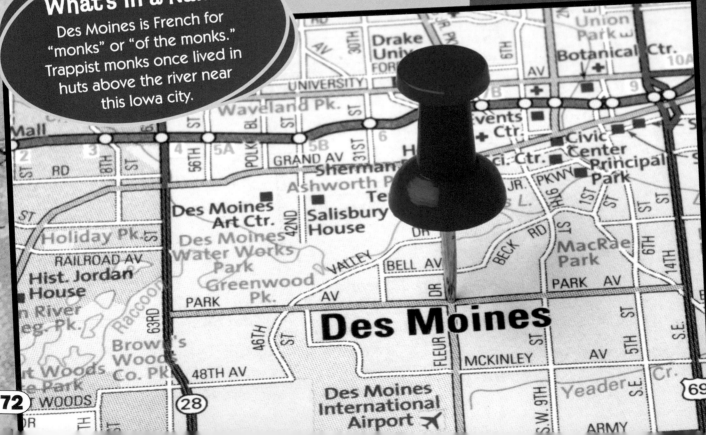

Des Moines

CITY RECORDS

Santa Fe, New Mexico, is the oldest city that's a U.S. state capital. It's also the highest state capital in altitude, at an elevation of 7,000 feet (2,133.6 m). Phoenix, Arizona, has the largest population (1.5 million) of all the state capitals. Montpelier, Vermont, has the fewest people—8,035, according to the 2000 Census. Austin, Texas, has the largest state capital building.

Vermont's state capitol, in Montpelier

UNITED STATES

TFK

Capital—Capitol
Did you know that a state's capital is the city, but its capitol is the building that houses its state government?

68 PUZZLE

Capital Ideas

Can you identify the capital and the state that will answer each clue?

1. Identify the one state capital whose name ends with the postal initials for the state that it's in. _____

2. Identify the one state capital whose name ends with the two letters that start the name of the state that it's in. _____

3. Identify the two state capitals that have names that completely include the names of their respective states. _____ _____

4. Identify the one state where the last four letters of the state's name begin the first four letters of its capital's name. _____

For a list of states, capitals, and postal abbreviations, see page 71.

73

NATIONAL PARKS

Units of the National Parks Service are found in every U.S. state except Delaware. The majority of national parks are west of the Mississippi River, and California has the most, at 23. Wyoming's Yellowstone National Park is the oldest national park in the country, established in 1872.

Each time Old Faithful erupts, it shoots out 3,700-8,400 gallons (14,000-32,000 L) of boiling water.

69 PUZZLE

Old Faithful

Old Faithful is located in Yellowstone National Park. Follow the directions to spell out what Old Faithful is:

1. Write out the name of the state that has Trenton for its capital.

2. Cross out the first word of that state's name. _____

3. Now change the first remaining letter to a g. _____

4. Switch the positions of the third and the sixth letters. _____

Love Those Hats!
The National Parks Service has been around since 1916. Wonder if park rangers will ever get different hats?

Range Rover

A mountain range in the western U.S. is hidden in these letters. To find it, you must cross the Rockies and the Ozarks. That is, you must cross out the letters in those two mountain range names from left to right to find the one that's hidden.

O
C
R
O
Z
A
C
S
A
K
S
C
K
R
A
I
E
K
D
A
S
S
E
S
S

RUGGED MOUNTAIN RANGES

Mountain ranges of various sizes can be found throughout the United States. In the east, the Appalachian Mountains run from Alabama and Georgia northward through Maine and into Canada. This range includes the Smoky Mountains and the Catskills. One of the most impressive ranges in the west is the Rockies. It extends over 2,980 miles (4,800 km), from British Columbia to New Mexico. Mt. McKinley, North America's highest peak, is located in the Alaskan Range.

Most national parks allow camping, and that's a wonderful way to enjoy the great outdoors!

WAY BACK WHEN

Ulysses S. Grant was President of the U.S. when Yellowstone became a national park.

Page 6 – Puzzle #1:
bear, bat, rat, beaver (You may have come up with others.)

Page 7 – Puzzle #2:
tarantula

Page 8 – Puzzle #3:
Here's one solution: (You may have found another.) NOTE: The Bs stand for Black frogs, and the Ws stand for White frogs.

BBB_WWW

BB_BWWW

BBWB_WW

BBWBW_W

BBW_WBW

B_WBWBW

_BWBWBW

WB_BWBW

WBWB_BW

WBWBWB_

WBWBW_B

WBW_WBB

W_WBWBB

WW__BWBB

WWWB__BB

WWW_BBB

Page 9 – Puzzle #4:
Polar bears live in the Arctic. Penguins only live in the southern hemisphere.

Page 10 – Puzzle #5:
Common Octopus

Page 11 – Puzzle #6:
The **gh** in "enough" is pronounced like f. The o in "women" is pronounced like a short i. The **tio** in "caution" is pronounced like sh. GHOTIO can be pronounced fish.

Page 12 – Puzzle #7:
A platypus has a bill like a duck, a tail like a beaver, and fur like an otter.

Page 13 – Puzzle #8:
koala, kangaroo, ostrich

Page 15 – Puzzle #9:
1. eyes, ears 2. head, heels
3. arm, leg

Page 15 – Puzzle #10:

Page 16 – Puzzle #11:
anosmia

Page 17 – Puzzle #12:
Upper left – Robert Pattinson, of Twilight; Upper right – Kristen Stewart, of Twilight; Lower left – Will Smith, of Hitch and Men in Blac Lower right – Daniel Radcliffe, of Harry Potter.

Page 19 – Puzzle #13:
eye, ear, toe, arm, leg, jaw, gum, hip, lip, rib (You may have come up with more.)

Page 19 – Puzzle #14:
1. brain 2. kidney
3. tendon 4. hand

Page 21 – Puzzle #15:
Phil + zipper – zr = Philippe; petal – AL + IT = Petit. The man's name was PHILIPPE PETIT.

Page 21 – Puzzle #16:
Florida. Its capital is Tallahassee.

Page 22 – Puzzle # 17:

Page 23 – Puzzle #18:
Lion = 50; Zebra = 52; Snake = 50; Wolf = 56. Wolf wins!

Page 24 – Puzzle #19:
Upper left – Cuba; Upper right – Brazil; Lower left – France; Lower right – Australia

Page 25 – Puzzle #20:
"All are ruled by Queen Elizabeth II.

age 27 – Puzzle #21:
ew Jersey

age 27 – Puzzle #22:
rincipality of Monaco

age 28 – Puzzle #23:
razil appears in the 5th column.

```
A  R  I  Z  B  L
L  B  Z  I  R  A
I  Z  R  L  A  B
B  A  L  R  Z  I
Z  L  B  A  I  R
R  I  A  B  L  Z
```

age 29 – Puzzle #24:

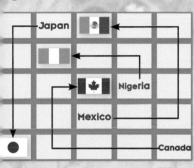

age 31 – Puzzle #25:

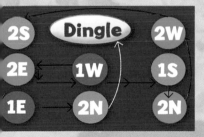

age 31 – Puzzle #26:
ma, Peru; Quito, Ecuador; Sucre,
olivia; Bogotá, Colombia; Brasilia,
razil; and Caracas, Venezuela. The
tters spell out EASTER ISLAND.

age 33 – Puzzle #27:
. photograph 2. busy 3. ninth
. Genesis. The underlined
arts of those words spell out
HOTOSYNTHESIS.

Page 33 – Puzzle #28:
Graph #3

Page 34 – Puzzle #29:
POLLUTION > PELLUTIEN >
PELUTILEN > PELUYILEN >
RELUYILEN > RELCYCLEN >
RECYCLE

Page 35 – Puzzle #30:
units, Saturn, punish

Page 36 – Puzzle #31:
Tyrannosaurus text

Page 37 – Puzzle #32:

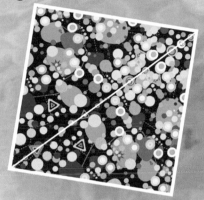

Page 38 – Puzzle #33:
The small blue fish on the left side
of the left picture is missing from
the right picture. The smaller tropical
fish, the tiny fish in the center, the
seashell in the lower left corner, and
the rock in the lower right-center of
the right picture are all missing from
the left picture.

Page 39 – Puzzle #34:
octopus

Page 40 – Puzzle #35:
Rushmore and Shasta

Page 41 – Puzzle #36:
Sherpa

Page 42 – Puzzle #37:
Henry Hudson's ship was
The Half Moon.

Page 43 – Puzzle #38:
rivers > riser > sire > sir > is > I

Page 44 – Puzzle #39:
deserts > desserts > stressed

Page 45 – Puzzle #40:
"Because of the sand which is there."
(Because of the sandwiches there.)

Page 46 – Puzzle #41:
sailing over the seven seas

Page 47 – Puzzle #42:
Huron, **O**ntario, **M**ichigan,
Erie, **S**uperior

Page 48 – Puzzle #43:
1. branches 2. leaves
3. bark 4. trunks

Page 49 – Puzzle #44:
1. maple 2. palm
3. cedar 4. pine

Page 50 – Puzzle #45:
ice > ace > act > apt >
opt > oat > cat

Page 51 – Puzzle #46:
1. ice fish 2. Ice Age
3. ice hockey 4. ice cream
5. iceberg 6. ice rink
7. ice chest 8. ice cube
9. ice pick 10. ice skate.
The letters in the blue boxes,
reading from top to bottom,
spell out FAHRENHEIT.

Page 52 – Puzzle #47:
Galileo

Page 53 – Puzzle #48:
tooth, **h**at, **o**wl, **m**oon,
apple, **s**un = Thomas.
egg, **d**og, **i**ce, **s**un, **o**wl, **n**et = Edison.
The first letters of these words spell
out THOMAS EDISON.

Page 54 – Puzzle #49:
The four-digit number is 3,975.
(3 is 1/3 of 9; 7 is two more than 5;
and 5 is two more than 3. Also,
3 + 9 + 7 + 5 = 24.)

Page 55 – Puzzle #50:
penicillin

Page 56 – Puzzle #51:
Freddie Highmore

Page 57 – Puzzle #52:
boxer, boxcar, ice box,
jukebox, tool box

Page 58 – Puzzle #53:
Hamm, from *Toy Story,* Mustafa,
the waiter from *Ratatouille,* and
Mack, from *Cars* all have the voice
of actor John Ratzenberger.

Page 59 – Puzzle #54:
bears, Ash, Monsters, Bob, Ice. The
first letters of all these words spell
out BAMBI, the title character of a
classic 1942 Disney animated movie.

Page 60 – Puzzle #55:
Spider-Man, Cyclops (from *X-Men*),
Superman, Batman, The Incredible
Hulk

Page 61 – Puzzle #56:
Batman patrols Gotham City;
Superman patrols Metropolis;
Spider-Man patrols New York City;
and The Flash patrols Central City.

Page 62 – Puzzle #57:
Contra was released by Vampire
Weekend; *Only by the Night* was
released by Kings of Leon; *Ocean
Eyes* was released by Owl City;
Transference was released by
Spoon; *Dark Horse* was released
by Nickelback; and *Leave this Town*
was released by Daughtry.

Page 63 – Puzzle #58:
Vanessa Hudgens

Page 64 – Puzzle #59:
cabbage

Page 65 – Puzzle #60:
Roc-A-Fella Records (The name is
similar to Rockefeller Center in New
York City, the site of New York's ice
skating rink, its annual Christmas tree,
and the address of TV's *30 Rock*.)

Page 66 – Puzzle #61:
569 = Pa**l**meiro; 630 = Gri**ff**ey;
762 = **B**onds; 714 = Ru**t**h. The
numbered letters spell out B – A – T
L – E – F – T – Y. "They all bat lefty."
They're all left-handed.

Page 67 – Puzzle #62:
From top to bottom, the words are:
backboard, **a**ssist, **s**hot, **k**ey, **e**lbow,
turnover, **b**lock, **a**lley-oop, **l**ayup, and
line. The letters in the gold boxes
down the left side, reading from top
to bottom, spell out BASKETBALL.

Page 68 – Puzzle #63:
For the Patriots: Brady's number
is 12, each touchdown is 6 points,
and each PAT is 1 point, so
12 ÷ 6 = 2 + 1 = 3. The Patriots
have lost 3 Super Bowls. For the
Giants: The Giants scored 3 points in
the 1st Quarter, there are 4 quarters
in a standard regulation football game,
Eli Manning's number is 10, and there

was 1 quarter of the game during
which neither team scored, so
3 X 4 = 12 – 10 = 2 – 1 = 1. The
Giants have lost 1 Super Bowl.

Page 69 – Puzzle #64:
One gold medal weighs 12 ounces.;
one silver medal weighs four
ounces; and one bronze medal
weighs two ounces; so one Olympic
gold medal weighs as much as six
Olympic bronze medals. (Actually
the weights of real Olympic medals
vary, depending on the design each
Olympic sponsoring city chooses.)

Page 70 – Puzzle #65:
Colorado, Maine, Indiana, Delaware,
and Arkansas. CO + ME IN DE + AR
= "Come in, Dear!"

Page 71 – Puzzle #66:
1. New York City, New York
2. New Orleans, Louisiana
3. Honolulu, Hawaii
4. Atlanta, Georgia
5. Oklahoma City, Oklahoma

Page 72 – Puzzle #67:
JUNE + AU = Juneau, Alaska.

Page 73 – Puzzle #68:
1. Albany, New York (NY)
2. Topeka, Kansas
3. Oklahoma City, Oklahoma
and Indianapolis, Indiana
4. Montpelier, Vermont

Page 74 – Puzzle #69:
1. New Jersey 2. Jersey
3. gersey 4. geyser

Page 75 – Puzzle #70:
CASCADES.